Anger Management

A Life-changing Resource For Anger Management, Stress Management, Emotional Wellness, And Effective Communication Skills

(The Definitive Resource For Managing Your Emotions And Achieving Inner Peace Anger Management: The Art Of Permanently Reducing Your Level Of Anger)

AntimoBalzano

TABLE OF CONTENT

Vital Information Regarding Stress 1

What Sets People Off In Their Anger? 9

What Is Management Of Anger? 46

How Should Your Anger Be Expressed? 81

Ten Strategies For Managing Your Anger 100

Be Aware Of Your Triggers 143

Furious Anger 163

Vital Information Regarding Stress

What general effects does it have on your wellbeing?

What are your coping mechanisms for anxiety and depression when you observe how your body responds to changes in your environment? Any issue can cause stress, including subpar work or academic performance, a big life transition, or a catastrophic event. Stress only has detrimental impacts; it largely has no positive ones.

It's important to observe how you respond to small and large demands to determine when you need assistance.

You should know a few things before we get too far into this subject.

1. Stress is a universal phenomenon.

Even the strongest people in the world experience actual stress; you are not alone. Stress comes in many forms, and each one harms one's physical and emotional wellbeing.

A stressor might occur once, briefly, or repeatedly throughout time. Some people are far more adept than others at handling stress and recovering from stressful situations.

These are a few instances of stress:

Frequent stress is brought on by the responsibilities of work, family, education, and other daily duties.

The majority of the time, certain issues in our lives cause worry and anxiety. A few of these issues include illness and possibly unhealthy relationships.

A major mishap, armed conflict, murder, assassination, or natural disaster where there is a risk of serious injury or death can cause traumatic stress. Severe stress exposure can cause uncomfortable, transient physical and emotional side effects, but most people recover on their own.

2. Not all stress is negative.

Stress causes the body to react by pulling away from potentially harmful objects.

In stressful conditions, your body tightens, your muscles beat faster, your respiration quickens and your brain becomes more active, all of which are survival-related reactions.

Sometimes, stress can be beneficial, particularly in everyday situations like interviews and tests with little risk of death.

3. Extended stress might be bad for your health.

Taking care of the consequences of ongoing stress can be challenging. Since it lasts longer, there is always a very low chance of recovery when someone experiences true long-term stress.

When the body is under continuous stress, those EXACT LIFE-SAVING processes can interfere with the immune, digestive, cardiovascular, sleep, and reproductive systems.

While some will only experience stomach problems, others may also experience headaches, insomnia, sadness, wrath, or irritability.

4. Stress management techniques exist.

Therefore, the following guidelines will assist you in efficiently managing your stress:

Be mindful. Understand the telltale signs of your body's stress response, which include difficulty falling asleep, increasing use of alcohol and other substances, irritability, depression, and poor energy.

Speak with a medical expert about your stress. Don't wait for the doctor to inquire about your stress management techniques. Start the discussion and ensure any new or developing health issues receive the proper medical care. Effective therapies can help if your stress negatively impacts your relationships or your ability to work.

Engage in regular exercise. Walking for 30 minutes daily might boost your health and elevate your mood.

Take part in something relaxing. Look into some wellness and relaxation practices, such as meditation, muscular relaxation, and breathing exercises. Plan these and other calming and healthful activities into your schedule regularly.

Take your recovery seriously. Don't give tomorrow or what to do next any thought. Remember to stay in the moment and know when to stop.

Keep your thoughts centered on the good. Focusing solely on your accomplishments rather than what you are missing out on will be beneficial. Your family can support you in maintaining your joy and optimism.

Take a clinical look at yourself.

5. If you're stressed out, get assistance.

As I mentioned earlier in this chapter, you should seek medical attention right away if you find yourself thinking about suicide or other harmful ideas. You'll receive advice from your doctor. There are resources available to help you locate a mental health specialist.

What Sets People Off In Their Anger?

Anger's spontaneity makes it challenging to pinpoint its origin or source. You can even feel as though your rage is suddenly building up. This is because rage always comes out so strong; it eliminates the source or catalyst and leaves you confused.

Usually, you are left with the fallout from your rage or the harm done without knowing what first sparked your wrath.

This kind of issue develops into a pattern that keeps happening, particularly in those with anger management issues.

I have witnessed situations where someone has an outburst of intense rage, and then the next moment, they cannot recall the initial cause. Sometimes, they don't realize the cause until after the explosion and regret the outcome.

It is not difficult for this to develop into a pattern or cycle. When anything triggers your anger, you respond violently at first, gain composure, realize your mistake, and repeat the same process in a different circumstance. Even worse, you don't try to figure out what's making you angry—instead, you just keep going in that unsettling direction.

Understanding the potential causes of your anger is critical to practice anger management techniques effectively. If you don't even know where something is coming from, it's tough to handle.

If you don't find and address the source of your anger, you won't be able to learn how to control it. For example, even if you pursue anger management, it will be challenging to manage your anger if it is being caused by stress and you are not addressing the stressors in your life. You'll keep getting upset for the silliest reasons as long as the stressors persist.

Whether on purpose or not, the people, places, and things you find yourself in usually make you angry. People are the most common source of anger out of these three (particularly those with whom you share intimate interactions). Family members, friends, lovers, and kids are a few of the individuals who could irritate or anger you all the time.

This makes sense because the people you interact with the most closely are typically your family, friends, and kids.

Moving on, aside from individuals or circumstances, several other things could be the source or trigger of your anger. It might not be because someone is continually bothering you or because the circumstances are typically upsetting if you are someone who becomes upset easily, regardless of how insignificant the scenario may be.

Often, the true cause of your anger may differ from what you believe. These are typically reasons you wouldn't even consider to be able to agitate you.

For example, you might feel something hit you when you walk inside your house after a long day at work. Upon entering the room, you discover that your 10-year-old child threw the object that struck you. Would you truly say that your child hurled something at you if you were to yell at them for hitting you?

Naturally, the reason you're angry may be that your child hurled something and hit you. If things hadn't occurred, how could you have become enraged and yelled at the child? But in reality, the cause of your ire is because you had a demanding workday.

You decided to take that as an opportunity to release some of the tension you were carrying from work. You certainly wouldn't mind if something was thrown at you if you were joyful, lively, and free-spirited when you returned home. Before entering, you may gather the child in your arms and engage in light play.

Therefore, sometimes, unknowingly, certain things will cause you to become angry. Below, I'll list and discuss some things that can provoke or produce your anger.

Early Life and Upbringing

A person's upbringing and youth greatly impact how they handle their anger and how they respond to it. In certain instances, a person's wrath as an adult stems from something they picked up along the way.

Many people learn about anger in ways that make it difficult or even impossible to control as adults as they grow up. It's possible that you were raised in a setting where people typically express their emotions by acting violently or aggressively. Thus, you are raised believing that expressing your anger this way is OK.

This thinking can make it difficult to recognize and control your anger. You thus become enraged over the little things. Even if you could have just gone up to them and discussed whatever they did, you might get upset because they did something you don't like. A phase of irrational outbursts may also occur when you find yourself in an unpleasant circumstance.

If you were raised to believe that suppressing your anger is the appropriate way to "express" it, then this is another way that your upbringing and childhood may have shaped how you respond to it. Many people were brought up with the idea that they should never file a complaint when they feel mistreated or cheated on. When they were kids, they were also disciplined for expressing anger.

This upbringing leads to the learning to repress anger, which is a big issue as an adult since it causes you to react improperly to uncomfortable situations. If you believe you shouldn't let your anger out, you could alternatively turn it inside on yourself.

You may have grown up witnessing your parents and other significant adults in your life behave irrationally when they are upset. You may now view rage as something extremely dangerous and terrifying as a result of this.

One of two things could occur: either you start to fear anger as a feeling, or you start to fear expressing your anger. This implies that you suppress your rage and refrain from speaking out when something upsetting occurs.

However, you can pick up this habit and begin behaving like the grownups you saw as a child. If you start to fear becoming upset, you can become furious again over things that have nothing to do with each other.

For instance, you can grow up believing that your parents' constant bickering and reconciliation is normal and begin to unconsciously or intentionally display similar habits in your relationships. If you and your partner do not argue within a week, you could feel uneasy because you think there might be a problem.

Various forms of rage and strategies for handling them

Our innate need to live and defend ourselves or what we believe to be right requires anger. People who are shy and don't easily become upset are often bullied and may always be afraid. Periodically expressing anger healthily is perfectly acceptable. As humans, it is only natural for us to desire to right a perceived wrong or stand up for the underdog, and sometimes this is justified. But rage can also be a very dangerous emotion that spirals out of control and turns destructive very rapidly. Anger management problems can have a detrimental effect on not just the person experiencing them but also those around them. The emotional, mental, and physical quality of your life will all significantly improve if you can learn to control and regulate your anger.

Various Forms of Anger

Inert

When someone exhibits passive anger, it might be interpreted as hostile, sarcastic, snide, pouting, or purposely ignoring someone. Since the person with anger management issues will do whatever they know or can to cause emotional distress to their target, it may come off as vile and malicious.

Internal

It is known as inward rage when someone represses or turns their fury within. Someone who self-harms or berates themselves when they are angry turns that rage inward. They frequently have a poor opinion of themselves and believe that nobody likes or understands them or that they are insufficient.

External

The most overt of the three is outward anger, which manifests as aggressiveness, physical harm, and/or verbal abuse that is frequently loud and blatant. When it comes to younger people, it frequently manifests as a full-blown temper tantrum in which the child may physically lash out or stamp and scream in frustration.

Chapter 3: Anger Management Techniques

We shall now get to the meat of the matter. Are you ready to learn the simple techniques that will allow you to control your anger? Make sure you follow the instructions we've provided; just reading them won't be helpful.

Games for controlling anger

There are tons of anger management games on the internet. Such games are easily found on the internet. Games are divided into various categories. It's critical to provide an outlet for your anger if you always hold it inside. Sometimes, having too much rage inside of you can result in violent outbursts that are very loud.

Therefore, you might try playing smash-em-up games to release some of your fury. Since all you have to do is beat the subjects, many games are based on this concept. Reports have shown that these games ultimately ended up encouraging a great deal of violence. It is up to you to choose the games and play them in a way that encourages the proper attitude within yourself.

Never make a snap decision when playing these games. Certain games demand you to concentrate on distinct topics, while others let you simply smash objects. The former will help you focus your positive energy in the proper places, while the latter is a good way to let out your frustration without endangering actual people.

Additionally, you can play games on your own without using the internet. We will discuss a handful of them here.

Joyful memories

You can write down every item that makes you happy in a notepad. Taking this step can help you ensure that you will recognize the things for which you are thankful. This awareness often calms you down enough to stop being angry.

resolving puzzles

As strange as it may sound, this is unquestionably one of the greatest games for controlling your rage. You can take your mind off what has been bothering you and divert it while immersed in solving problems. When you are completely engaged in anything, you can ensure you are not wasting time being upset, which will benefit you in many ways.

Play a humorous scene.

Even though this is arguably the most straightforward Fury game, it works quite well. Everybody has a few favorite movie or book sequences. Try acting out a humorous scene if you lose control of your wrath. While a humorous moment is not essential, it should have a positive significance. By doing this, you'll be distracted while allowing positive energy and vibration to infuse.

So, don your acting caps and go steal the show once more.

Meditating

The benefits of meditation are limitless. Making sure you are putting money into the power of meditation is crucial. The science that teaches you how to control and manage your emotions is called meditation. People adept at meditation are frequently observed to have far greater mental tranquility.

Meditation has to be one of the best strategies you can use to control your anger problems. When deciding to meditate, you should follow a few guidelines, which we shall outline for you.

• You should always aim to meditate for an hour after waking up early. You must do this since meditation requires a new lease on life. It is well known that the early morning hours are full of positive energy, which will help you focus much more intensely.

- Be mindful not to rush through your meditation sessions. The greatest way to experience the benefits of meditation is to take your time and practice with mental clarity.

- Take your time and start slowly; hurrying things along will never produce the results you're looking for. Deep breathing exercises should be your first choice if you are a beginner. You must focus on your breathing throughout this exercise. Take a deep breath and then release it as soon as possible to assist you in getting rid of any negative thoughts.

- It is important that you put in the appropriate amount of effort during these workouts. Another important thing to remember is to avoid having different thoughts running through your mind while deep breathing. The goal of meditation will be undermined if you let your mind get distracted by other ideas.

- You should make an even greater effort to regulate your breathing daily. Gaining more control over your inner mind's operations is crucial. There's a wide range of how long you can maintain breath control. Being able to regulate your breathing for an extended time indicates that you will also be able to monitor your emotions.

- You must then intensify your training after you have achieved complete control over your breathing movements. As you should preferably strive to focus on something and draw energy from the same, you should go on to harder workouts. You can attempt to focus on a stationary point in space or visualize a scene and then focus on it. Whatever you decide, the main concept is to extract energy from the same. Positive energy can banish your anger, which can also assist you in appropriately managing your anger management problems.

- When it comes to your meditation sessions, you must arrive on time. You can't possibly afford to tamper with your sessions. Thus, make sure you dedicate the appropriate amount of time and effort. You must make a plan; unless it is an emergency that cannot wait, you should not skip your meditation sessions.

The effects will eventually become apparent after you put all of these suggestions into practice. We want you to know that it is unrealistic to anticipate changes right away, so we will be honest with you. You must put up your best effort for an extended amount of time to control your anger, as it is a behavioral issue.

Because it helps to calm your mind, meditation is well known to be a very powerful tool for managing your anger. Your heightened emotional state is primarily the reason for your rage since it makes it difficult for you to maintain control over the situation.

Therefore, you should make sure that you set aside the appropriate amount of time for meditation, and the changes will manifest within a week or perhaps even a month.

The energy equilibrium

Do you think the energy theory is true? According to one hypothesis, everything occurring in and around us is an energy change. You will be more successful if you surround yourself with positive energy; thus, it is crucial.

According to the energy hypothesis, all the molecules in your body will align when you are at peace, allowing you to feel more in tune with your overall well-being. When you're uncomfortable and uneasy, anger comes out. You must practice the many techniques for balancing the energy within your mind since the collision of energy molecules within your body occurs randomly and haphazardly.

#11 Yoga is marketed as a technique for people of all ages to relax and relieve tension. Yoga aims to unite the mind and body. There are many different types of yoga, such as Anusara, Bikram, and hot yoga. The main way to do this is by raising a person's awareness of their body and breath.

Research has been conducted to investigate the impact of yoga on an individual's general psychological well-being. According to the findings, yoga can be utilized to elevate mood and may even have antidepressant properties that lessen anxiety and melancholy. More research must be done to fully understand the efficacy of yoga in enhancing mental health in individuals.

Thus far, research seems to show that yoga's capacity to lessen anxiety and stress arises from its impact on the neurological system and the body's reaction to stress. Additionally, yoga may help lower heart rate and blood pressure. It's feasible that practicing yoga will also increase gamma-aminobutyric acid levels, as this neurotransmitter is likewise decreased in people with mood disorders.

#12 One of the key strategies for lowering stress is to give the body permission to achieve mindfulness. Practicing mindfulness helps people stay present and compels them to give up worrying thoughts.

Additionally, practicing mindfulness can assist in combating an individual's internalized negative beliefs related to stress and anxiety. Additionally, mindfulness has been connected in recent research to higher levels of self-esteem, which can lessen the symptoms of anxiety and despair.

#13 Spending quality time with a significant other is another excellent method of stress relief. Something as easy as sharing a kiss, embrace, or sex before bed can help someone feel at ease and ease.

According to the findings, those who have positive physical body contact release oxytocin and have lower cortisol levels. Blood pressure and heart rate are two physical signs of stress that the body's natural reaction reduces.

Remarkably, chimpanzees have also been shown to comfort their stressed-out buddies through pleasant physical touch; humans are not the only animals who do this.

#14 Many individuals know that you may express your emotions through music. A person can use music to help any emotion achieve its pinnacle, whether it be happiness, anger, or sadness. Music and stress might be related in the same way. Research has indicated that music can induce complete relaxation in the body.

Because calming music naturally lowers blood pressure and pulse rate, listening to slow instrumental music might make a person more relaxed. Additionally, listening to music can lessen the body's release of stress hormones.

Listening to music one enjoys might be soothing, but certain genres, such as Celtic, Native American, and classical music, are especially helpful. Both relaxation and meditation music, including natural sounds, can be soothing.

#15 Breathing techniques are a fantastic method to quickly teach the body how to achieve full-body tranquility.

The body releases stress chemicals during the "fight or flight" response, causing people to physically react with symptoms including elevated heart rate, fast breathing, and constricted blood vessels. To maintain homeostasis, the parasympathetic nervous system must establish itself.

A breathing technique that induces a controlled relaxation response is one of the greatest ways to do this.

Abdominal breathing exercises help one stay focused, generate new energy, and relax physically and mentally. To perform the exercise, one must inhale through the nose and permit the diaphragm to expand—not the chest.

A person's heart and respiratory system can be balanced using paced respiration. This encourages the body's stress-reduction systems to become active.

The diaphragm, a crucial muscle involved in breathing daily, is strengthened when someone practices diaphragmatic breathing, commonly called belly breathing. The primary breathing method utilized in relaxation and meditation is this specific one.

Diaphragmatic breathing has several advantages, including lowering blood pressure, lowering stress hormones, lowering heart rate, and enabling the body to withstand high exertion levels.

To ensure the user is using the technique correctly, any breathing exercises can be obtained online and through phone apps.

#16 Pets can help their owners cope with stress and anxiety in ways other than emotional support animals. Research indicates that an individual's general mood can be enhanced by spending time with their pet.

It's possible that engaging with a pet causes the brain's oxytocin molecule to be released. The substance is intended to enhance a person's spirits.

A pet can provide a person with a sense of purpose, keep them active, and provide company, to name a few particular ways in which they can assist in reducing stress.

There are easy strategies to lessen a person's overall pressure and stress levels, even if stress can occur at work and home. The recommendations' primary objective is to divert attention from the primary cause of stress. Reducing stress will also assist a person in leading a more balanced lifestyle.

#17 A person genuinely gives themselves a chance to lower their stress levels when they can maintain a balanced diet. According to studies, a healthy diet helps a person create a more resilient foundation for their body because some meals also lower inflammation and oxidation. It's also commonly known that eating healthful foods might aid in avoiding gaining weight.

The problem then becomes finding the time to cook a balanced dinner. It can be difficult to prepare a nutritious dinner when one is extremely stressed; therefore, takeout is typically the preferred option. The amount of beneficial nutrients that a home-cooked meal can offer can be reduced by dining out. One way to address the issue of unhealthy eating is for someone to establish a pattern that includes prepping healthful meals.

According to studies, people are more likely to select healthier foods at home instead of dining out. People can guarantee that they always have wholesome meals by purchasing nutrient-dense items regularly. Many foods, such as fruits, nuts, and high-fiber cereals, can be frozen or dried.

What Is Management Of Anger?

Anger is a feeling that both adults and children experience. When something or someone negatively interferes with an individual, it might anger them. Anger is a typical reaction to such a circumstance. Conversely, angst might be described as a moderate to severe irritation. Depending on the person, the situation, and emotions, anger can make someone enraged or even furious. Anger can affect people in different ways. Some people lash out or are quite protective. Some try to bottle up their negative emotions and hurt and keep their fury to themselves. At the same time, some became careless and even abusive. If anger isn't controlled, it can be quite harmful.

Rage management is the control of rage. Some people are blind to their major anger issues. Naturally, something happens to irritate and anger someone. People who struggle to acknowledge their emotions and accept responsibility for their actions frequently engage in the blame game. They find it difficult to accept that the situation is their fault. There's always someone or something to blame. Their outbursts of anger are invariably rooted in something else. These people might benefit from a few lessons in anger management. But they must accept their actions and reactions for what they are: differences.

When anger management is recommended, a lot of people with anger management problems find it depressing. Not being able to accept their problem stops them from getting the assistance they need. When someone keeps going down a path where they act out and become angry all the time, it will eventually lead to major problems. Without proper management, this person is likely to suffer from loss— losing their identity, their job, their family, and their own.

Convincing the person with anger management issues is essential; anger management is not meant to be a form of punishment but rather to assist them in leading better lives. Anger management is intended to assist each person in working through their issues and understanding the reasons behind their outbursts. Additionally, it teaches the person to control their anger and not let it consume them.

Anger destroys not just the angry person but everyone and everything around them. Anger control can transform this and ensure an individual's normal, healthy life.

Myths and Reality Regarding Anger and Anger Management

- Myth: I shouldn't try to "resist" my rage. It's healthy to let it out and vent.

Fact: While it's true that ignoring and suppressing anger is unhealthy, venting isn't any better. It is unnecessary to "let out" your anger aggressively to prevent blowing up. Angry outbursts and tirades just fuel the flames and exacerbate your anger management issues.

- Myth: I can learn to respect and get what I want by using anger, aggression, and intimidation.

Reputation doesn't stem from mistreating other people. People may be afraid of you, but they won't respect you if you can't control yourself or handle uncomfortable situations. If you speak respectfully, people will be more inclined to listen to you and accommodate your requirements.

- Myth: I'm powerless over myself. Anger is not something you have control over.

Fact: You have some control over how you express your anger, but you can't always control your situation or how it makes you feel. Furthermore, you can express your anger without physical or verbal abuse. You always have a choice about how you respond, even if someone is putting pressure on your buttocks.

Where Does Anger Originate?

Many ask: where does anger originate? The solution is not as complex as the complexity of anger management.

Anger stems from our innate and natural desire to defend ourselves. When we become furious, our natural reaction is usually fear or a perceived lack of control. Anger is a fundamental defense mechanism that typically manifests when we are rejected, attacked, threatened, or confronted with an event for which we are unprepared.

Different things make different people angry. What enrages you might not enrage your neighbor. This is because you face a different set of threats than your neighbors.

- Refusal

Rejection produces rage. If you're wondering where the rage comes from, consider how you felt the last time you weren't hired for a position you thought you did a good job interviewing for.

Consider a failed relationship, a divorce, or any other period when you felt excluded or abandoned. Anger in any of those scenarios is a natural emotion. Anger can cover up other emotional responses, such as insecurity or a loss of identity.

Anyone would rather be angry than unwanted or unloved. When you begin to feel angry following a rejection, acknowledge those emotions and immediately strive to do something that gives you a sense of support and love.

Spend time with long-time friends, pay a compassionate visit to a patient, or engage in an activity you know you're skilled at.

- Assault

A physical attack will frequently trigger an instant defense reaction in addition to rage. You might be expected to react negatively if someone hurts you without apparent reason, and your first reaction might be to strike back.

The anger that surfaced when someone tried to hurt you was there to protect you. Your emotional response has to be fueled by a bit of additional adrenaline when your physical safety is in jeopardy.

You will feel enraged even if the attack is not physical. When someone disparages your ideas or openly criticizes anything you've done, you will become enraged and want to strike back. Being true to yourself is a natural and appropriate way to express who you are.

It's a healthy way to respond to adversity. However, fighting back excessively won't make you feel any better. Use your anger to defend yourself when necessary, but do not allow that anger to get the better of you and cause needless physical aggressiveness.

- Insufficient Control

Everyone likes to feel in control of their lives, but anger may surface when that control is lacking.

Simple things out of your control, like canceledflights, can cause major life events like serious illnesses in your family or losing your job.

You might act out less than productive, such as yelling, blaming others, and becoming irrationally angry. Once you understand where the anger originates, take a minute to step back from it and understand that becoming angry won't give you any more control over an already extremely difficult situation.

Are you feeling too enraged?

There are psychological tests that measure your level of rage, your susceptibility to upsets, and your ability to manage your anger. However, if you have a problem controlling your anger, you probably already know it. If you realize your actions are terrible and uncontrollable, you might need help finding better coping skills.

According to psychologist Jerry Deffenbacher, Ph......., who specializes in anger management, certain people are more "hotheaded" than others; they get angry faster and more intensely than the average person. Some people are always upset and furious but don't show it in blatantly dramatic ways. Not only do people who become upset readily swear and throw objects, but they can also withdraw socially, mope, or get sick.

Those who become angry easily tend to have a low tolerance for frustration or believe they shouldn't have to deal with irritation, difficulty, or inconvenience. They can't take things as they are and get particularly angry when anything seems unjust.

What makes these people who they are? Numerous distinct things. There is evidence that certain children are inherently irritable, touchy, and fast to become angry. These features manifest from a very young age, suggesting a genetic or physiological component may be at play. An additional component could be sociocultural. It is common to view expressing rage as negative; instead, we are taught that expressing other emotions, such as depression and anxiety, is acceptable. As a result, we never learn how to control or constructively use it.

Research has shown a connection between conduct and family history. Those who are easily offended usually come from dysfunctional, chaotic homes where emotional expression is difficult.

Does "letting it all hang out" have any advantages?

Psychologists today consider this idea to be dangerous. Some use this theory to justify their mistreatment of others. Research indicates that expressing your anger visibly doesn't help you or the person you are angry with resolve the problem; instead, it only helps to increase hatred and aggression.

It's critical to recognize your anger triggers and develop coping strategies around them to keep yourself from losing your cool.

How to manage your rage

Unwinding

Anger can be reduced with two simple relaxation techniques: deep breathing and visualization of peaceful imagery. You can acquire relaxation techniques through books and online courses that you can use whenever you'd like. If you are in a relationship with a hot-tempered partner, it could be a good idea for both of you to learn these tactics.

You can try these simple steps:

Imagine your "gut" as the place where your breath comes from.

Repeat soothing phrases like "take it easy" or "relax" slowly. Say it out loud to yourself while inhaling deeply.

Use photographs to bring back a peaceful recollection or moment from your mind. You may feel calmer after doing simple, slow yoga-style motions.

Apply these techniques regularly. Learn to employ them on autopilot when faced with difficult situations.

Different Kinds of Anger

Anger disorders come in many different forms, and most people who struggle with controlling their anger frequently suffer from them. Numerous psychologists have published on a wide spectrum of anger disorders, most of which are in disagreement with one another. To avoid conflict, nevertheless,

I shall limit my discussion of rage to the commonly acknowledged varieties.

Indifference to rage

People prone to passive anger frequently aren't even aware they are upset. When you exhibit passive rage, your feelings include sarcasm, cruelty, or indifference. These individuals have typically been observed participating in specific activities, such as missing work or school or even isolating themselves from other people. Additionally, they do poorly, particularly in professional and social settings. Even though they might not be aware of it or even be able to defend their behavior, they might appear to be attempting to harm themselves to others.

Given that rage can be repressed, this could make it difficult to identify. The only thing that may be encouraging in this circumstance is figuring out what emotion is driving your behavior so that you can effectively confront the source of your rage and find a solution.

Aggressive anger

Even though they might not always be aware of the underlying reason for their anger, people who feel this rage are typically conscious of their emotional states. In other cases, you will witness them using scapegoats as a focal point for their violent outbursts. This simply makes addressing the underlying problem more difficult. You should be aware that volatile or retaliatory rage is an example of how aggressive anger presents itself. This may result in bodily harm to other individuals or their belongings. So that you can effectively control symptoms when they arise and deal with them more positively and constructively, you must learn to identify anger triggers.

Anger with assertiveness

This is among the most productive ways people channel their rage toward making a change for the better. This implies that you choose to express your anger in a way that affects change without necessarily being harmful or upset instead of avoiding conflict or holding it inside.

Most people believe that assertive rage is a strong motivator that enables people to fulfill their ambitions.

Anger behavior

This is the type of rage that frequently manifests physically. People who experience this form of fury frequently feel so overcome by their emotions that they lash out in a rage at objects as a way to vent it. It is frequently highly unpredictable and has a detrimental effect on the course that their lives take after that, primarily due to the interpersonal and legal ramifications.

You must give yourself some time to cool down when you're this angry so that you don't do anything you'll regret forever. To ensure that you regain control, you can accomplish this by removing yourself from the scenario and engaging in self-talk.

persistent rage

This is frequently a persistent, more widespread hatred toward other people. One may become enraged with oneself. It frequently comes with a tendency to become agitated, which is typically extended and may eventually hurt your wellness.

The best way to manage this type of rage is to give it some thought and consider potential triggers. By allowing yourself to go through a phase of forgiveness for any previous sins, you can better cope with your inner conflict once you have recognized the trigger. This forgiveness process is essential to deal with the hurt and irritation you may have been holding on to.

Judgmental anger

This is a justified rage that frequently targets an injustice that is felt to have occurred. Even while this kind of hatred is acceptable since it assumes a moral superiority posture, it might make friends feel uneasy by simply invalidating their beliefs.

The greatest method to deal with this kind of rage is to commit to investigating many scenarios, even though they may appear straightforward on the surface but have deeper complexity.

Anger that abuses oneself

This kind of fury is commonly known as shame-based anger. This implies that if you've been experiencing a great deal of hopelessness and humiliation, you can internalize those emotions and use self-harm or harsh self-talk as a way to release the pent-up rage inside of you. Others may turn to substance misuse and disordered eating, which can lead to low self-esteem and social estrangement.

You must use cognitive reframing strategies to confront and eliminate any self-defeating thoughts you may be having to deal with this rage. Also, you might discover that practicing attentive meditation helps you control your impulses.

Anger expressed verbally

This kind of rage is frequently perceived as psychological abuse meant to harm the people who are thought to be the source of the anger in the first place. Among other verbal signs, this rage may manifest as threats, mockery, criticism, blaming, and yelling. Following this outburst, regret and feelings of shame follow.

You must consider carefully before speaking to manage your wrath. While it may be tempting to say anything out loud in the heat of the moment, resisting the urge to do so is the key to controlling your anger. You'll find that with practice, you can effectively stop the impulse toward verbal abuse and swap it out with an authoritative statement.

6. Persistent Anger

Chronic anger is frequently directed against others, situations, or even yourself, which can lower self-esteem. It can occasionally do a considerable deal of harm without being discovered.

Regardless, persistent anger is an addiction that will ruin your relationships in addition to wreaking havoc on your physical and mental health if you don't seek help.

You'll soon find yourself alone with your rage as everyone around you grows weary of having to tread carefully.

An ongoing, low-level sense of rage, contempt, irritation, and impatience is the hallmark of chronic anger. As previously mentioned, it can apply to specific situations, other people, or you. Because of your anger management style, you may find it difficult to communicate and manage your needs, which can negatively impact your relationships, anxiety levels, and general well-being.

7. Excessive Fury:

Being extremely angry might erratically affect your emotional health in the long run. This kind of rage arises, especially when you can't find a means to express your feelings or communicate. It may manifest when something reaches a "limit," or certain situations, emotions, or interactions have overpowered your ability to control anger and tension.

Overwhelming fury might appear as an unanticipated outburst of annoyance and contempt after a protracted period of repression. Although everyone's display of overwhelming fury seems different, it often arises suddenly and may be preceded by an upsetting event.

8. Anger with judgment:

Judgmental anger is typically a reaction to some perceived slight, another person's flaws (if you believe they influence you), or a betrayal of you or another individual. It is identified by people's core beliefs, which are their basic worldviews or worldviews; these beliefs are typically related to feeling better than others or more regrettable than them, which makes you judge them and get enraged over their actions or words.

It appears that the main cause of judgmental anger is what people refer to as "justified fury," which occurs when you or another person becomes enraged about a perceived slight or injustice. This form of fury can equally seem to be putting others down or ranting over an apparent injustice. This can negatively affect your relational corporations and restrict your capacity to keep an emotional support system. What's more, you can confront sensations of despair and low self-esteem.

9. Anger Based on Pain: This is often a kind of anger that hides pain, suffering, or even serious despair.

Similar to dread, the hardest emotions to cope with are agony and grief. For some people, anger is easier to express since, even if only briefly, it can make you feel strong, but melancholy and depression can make you feel weak.

Anger might occasionally feel like the primary tool of choice when suffering engulfs you in melancholy.

Whatever the case, the reality is that it makes things worse. This kind of rage ignores the primary source of annoyance and causes additional suffering, such as regret, loneliness, and guilt.

10. Passive-Aggressive Anger: This is a kind of rage that, to put it mildly, manifests itself as suppression of your feelings and an attempt to avoid a variety of conflicts. If everything else is equal, it comes out in small ways, like sardonic comments or acts of blind aggression towards the person you're angry with, like 'neglecting' to fill up your car with petrol when you know your spouse won't be able to make it to work each morning.

Passive and aggressive aggression is also an avoidant form of expression. It's usually dangerous because rage frequently lowers your self-esteem. Your relationships may be impacted by passive-aggressive fury.

It can also take the form of verbal or physical abuse, as well as emotional repression and conflict avoidance. This could appear as mocking, a purposeful lack of response, or distant, aggressive comments (such as, "I like your outfit, even though it doesn't fit you").

The most common passive-aggressive fury is verbal, which can appear as closed-off nonverbal communication or persistent procrastination at work.

11. Righteous Anger: This is a constructive kind of rage. There's a purpose to this fury.

This kind of rage motivates you to take action, such as righting a wrong or protecting the defenseless, innocent, and defenseless. It also improves the state of the globe.

12. Volatile Anger: Sometimes referred to as "unexpected/sudden anger," volatile anger is a dangerous form of rage. It can occur when someone gets irritated, no matter how minor, and explodes, either physically or verbally, sometimes turning gruesome. The person finds it difficult to process,

convey, and articulate their thoughts when angry.

Volatile rage might shift from the situation to shock at real or imagined slights. It can involve shouting, shrieking, hurling objects, and physical aggressiveness and is usually disastrous. You might not be able to maintain consistent, solid, and trustworthy relationships if you are angry in this way.

How Should Your Anger Be Expressed?

Everybody gets furious occasionally, but everyone handles anger differently. Jane discovered a romantic message from a different woman on her spouse's phone. She chose to face her spouse because she was furious. Despite acknowledging that he had an extramarital affair, the husband expressed regret and asked Jane for forgiveness.

To preserve her marriage, Jane repressed her rage. She kept repeating the message she saw repeatedly in her head, which caused the anger to grow over time. Later on, she had a disease and depressed herself. I'm attempting to say we should never hold back from expressing our displeasure.

When upset, we frequently lash out, criticize, withdraw, and speak poorly about the person who wronged us. We may come to regret the decisions we made when we are furious. But remember that once we speak, we cannot take back our words. Anger can be expressed in constructive ways that don't harm us or the people around us. The following are some more effective ways to communicate anger:

Speak in an easygoing manner.

Instead of speaking angrily or raising your voice, people are more inclined to listen to a reasoned argument. Someone's response will depend on how you approach them. Someone will react violently or walk out on you if you speak aggressively.

Speak impartially.

When we are upset, we should watch what words we use since they affect how the other person responds. Words like "never" and "always" are inappropriate when we are upset.

For instance, the generalization "You never care about my feelings." Rather, you should be more explicit and highlight why you believe the other person doesn't care about your feelings. Rather than labeling someone as nasty or nasty, tell them what happened to you and how you feel about it.

Identify your needs.

You must be clear about your expectations of the individual who injured you. To achieve this, ask yourself the following questions:

Would you prefer that the individual behave differently going forward?

Do you want the offender to accept responsibility for their errors and extend an apology?

Do you want the individual to assist you in resolving the current issue?

Share your ideas and feelings with the other person and what enraged you. Describe what you expect from that individual and how satisfying those expectations will impact your relationship. We show ourselves and others respect when we act in this composed manner.

Pay attention to the here and now.

It is simple to bring up previous transgressions when you are upset, and doing so will just fuel your rage. Moving on from the past and addressing the current problem is a good idea.

Strike a punching bag.

You can hit a gym bag while walking to the gym and visualize you hitting the person who injured you. Strike it hard enough to feel your body relax and release stress. When you're calm, you can then return and resolve your problem.

Exercise patience and pay attention to what the other person has to say.

You ought to be able to offer the other person an opportunity to clarify. You ought to be allowed to hear their justifications for the things they did that caused you harm.

Put it in writing.

Some folks find that putting their rage on paper helps them feel better. You are free to write down your thoughts and plans. It's been claimed that writing nasty things down is preferable to speaking them aloud.

The Impact of Anger on Your Life and Health

Relationships can be strengthened, and mutual understanding can be fostered by constructive ways to express anger, such as being aggressive. However, anger can lead to social and physiological issues if it becomes a habit.

Therefore, the following are some of the reasons you might want to look into productive coping mechanisms if you frequently suffer from rage issues:

Anger Can Increase Your Heart Disease Risk

Studies have indicated that chronic anger can result in heart issues. According to medical research, individuals with higher impulsivity are twice as likely to have heart issues than those with lower impulsivity.

An elevated heart rate is one of the physiological signs of chronic rage.

Research in the medical field has consistently demonstrated that those with poor anger management skills have a higher risk of stroke than those with less anger. According to one such study, during a few hours following an angry outburst, there is a threefold increased risk of stroke caused by a blood clot in the brain. Additionally, reports suggest that after an emotional argument, those with brain artery aneurysms are six times more likely to rupture the aneurysm.

Even though you might find these figures startling, you shouldn't be concerned if you struggle with anger management. By taking the initiative to discover constructive coping mechanisms for your anger management issues, you may simply avoid these situations.

Anger Boosts Nervousness

It might be time for you to discover a workable answer if you consistently battle with anger management problems. This is because anger has been connected to heightened anxiety in people. Studies also show that people who are frequently angry are more likely to feel hostile and dissatisfied with their circumstances, which makes their anxiety issues worse.

Anger Can Make Your Immune System Weaker

To benefit your health, you should discover a method to calm down if you lose your temper too easily. This is because, if left untreated, anger management disorders may make you more susceptible to sickness. Research has demonstrated that furious behaviors and reactions might result in a considerable decrease in immunoglobulin A antibody levels, which is critical for a functioning immune system.

If you are someone who struggles with anger management all the time, you should take immediate action to safeguard your immune system by learning good coping mechanisms.

Anger Can cause Depression.

Numerous researches have shown a link between Depression and chronic rage. It has been demonstrated that people who suppress their anger are more likely to overthink things, which frequently results in Depression and other mental health problems. You might want to redirect your attention to something you enjoy doing or learning about if your rage is causing you to overthink things. This will give you time to collect yourself to confront your anger with courage and clarity.

Anger Can Shorten Your Life Quite a Bit

Stress and overall health and well-being have been linked in medical research for a long time. Individuals who experience constant stress are less likely to prioritize self-care than those who lead pleasant and fulfilling lives. Excessive anger has been proven in studies to dramatically raise the body's stress hormone levels. One's lifespan may be significantly shortened if this spirals out of hand. Because of this, a lot of health professionals who work as counselors stress the need for people to be more honest about their anger and find constructive ways to cope with it rather than holding it inside.

Anger Can Contribute to Obesity

Obesity and weight issues in men and women have been related to long-term stress and anger. Anger-related stress obesity typically manifests as weak arms and legs, a large amount of abdominal fat, and a bloated feeling. It is critical to understand that because a variety of stress hormones are typically the root cause of the issue, stress obesity cannot be effectively addressed with standard methods like diet and exercise alone. Medication, diet, and stress management are crucial to tackle this issue.

Anger Can Result in Drug Dependency

While it is acceptable to feel irritated accidentally once in a while, being angry all the time might result in drug abuse and addiction. According to studies, those who struggle to control their anger are more prone to overuse drugs and alcohol.

Although some people tend to use alcohol or other drugs as a way to cope with their anger, this is typically not a good idea. Repressing anger and irritation with drugs or alcohol can set off a vicious cycle of violence that can have catastrophic consequences for the user. Consequently, you must take the required actions to manage your anger.

Anger May Cause Desire Loss

If you've watched any romance-themed films or television series, you've undoubtedly seen portrayals of couples that argue vehemently one minute and then make passionate love the next. Although this idealization might work in films, most people's realities are very different from this. Anger and closeness don't mix well for a lot of people. For this reason, when they're upset, a lot of people stop wanting to have sex with their spouse.

Your anger management issue may be the root of your decreased excitement for intimacy with your partner.

Anger can hurt other aspects of your life besides your physical health. First of all, feeling angry can seriously undermine your self-worth and confidence. Even while having violent outbursts as a way to express your anger may feel good at the moment, failing to effectively manage your anger problem can have negative effects, including regret, shame, and embarrassment. This might lead to a decline in your self-esteem, which would send you into a downward spiral of guilt and resentment towards yourself and others.

Furthermore, having uncontrollable rage can seriously harm your marriage, friendships, and family ties. While it's necessary for there to be healthy ways for people to express their anger, acting out in fits of wrath can breed mistrust and anxiety in a partnership. For example, if you frequently lose your temper at your partner or child for doing something you don't agree with, they could be less likely to confide in you about their problems. As a result, each genuine relationship must be built on a shaky basis.

Suppressing your anger can be just as harmful to your relationships as lashing out, which is a destructive method to deal with rage. Resentment, which comes from holding your anger inside, can cause a rift and hostility between you and your loved ones. Moreover, rage can lead to overanalyzing and incorrect conclusions, creating needless stress and instability in your relationships.

Therefore, you should try to talk to your loved ones and find constructive ways to let your anger out. This promotion of trust and understanding will make your relationships stronger and more satisfying.

Unchecked rage could negatively impact your career, which can also affect other aspects of your life. If you're like most people, the workplace is the one area where you are most likely to experience and deal with rage. This is a result of the intense performance-related pressure that exists in offices.

Ten Strategies For Managing Your Anger

Controlling your temper might be difficult.

Are you angry when someone cuts you out of traffic during rush hour? When your child is uncoordinated, does your blood pressure skyrocket? Anger is a common and surprisingly stable emotion. Positively handling it is important in every event. An out-of-control anger can harm your relationships and your general well-being.

Are you ready to resolve your rage issues? Take a look at these ten suggestions for managing rage first.

1. Consider your words before speaking

It's not difficult to say something you'll regret later, even if it seems out of the blue. Before you say something, give yourself a few seconds to collect your thoughts. Permit others who are involved in the situation to follow suit.

2. Share your interests when you're at ease.

Express your wrath in a calm, assured way while you're thinking clearly. Without hurting or trying to manipulate others, clearly and directly state your wants and interests.

3. Engage in physical activity

Engaging in physical labor can help reduce stress, which can lead to emotional disturbances. In the unlikely event that you feel your fury rising, go for a vigorous run or stroll. Alternatively, spend some effort on other enjoyable proactive projects.

4. Have a rest.

Kids don't always need breaks. When you are experiencing generally distressing circumstances, give yourself little breaks. A few moments of quiet time could help you feel better and more prepared to handle the inevitable event without being upset or angry.

5. Identify potential fixes

Instead of focusing on what was driving you crazy, try to resolve the primary issue that needs to be resolved. Is your child's disorganized room upsetting you? Shut the door behind you. Is your partner always running late for dinner? Arrange dinners for a later time. Alternatively, you could agree to eat alone a few times a week. Recognize that some things are also essentially out of your control. Try to think practically about what you can and cannot alter. Recognize that anger won't solve anything and can even worsen it.

6. Adhere to the "I" statement

Critiquing or pointing out flaws could make things more stressful. Illustrate the problem with "I" explanations. Be mindful and clear. Say, instead of "You never do any housework," something like, "I'm disturbed that you passed on the table without proposing to assist with the dishes."

7. Aim to let go of grudges

Forgiving someone who has displeased you could benefit you both from the situation and strengthen your bond.

8. Laugh to relieve tension

Relaxing can help to reduce stress. Use comedy to help you face your frustrations and, possibly, any irrational beliefs about how things should be. Avoid making fun of others, as this can exacerbate the problem and make you feel awful.

9. Work on your ability to relax

Set unwinding powers to action when your emotion spirals out of control. Engage in deep breathing exercises, visualize a relaxing location, or repeat a calming phrase or word, like "Relax." You can also use other methods to decompress and rejuvenate, such as listening to music, journaling, or doing a few poses in yoga.

10. Recognize when to seek assistance

Sometimes, it's a test to learn how to control anger. Seek assistance if you are experiencing anger management problems. Maybe your outrage comes across as extreme, causes you to act in ways you regret, or hurts those around you.

Abuse of Alcohol

One common feeling that most individuals experience is anger. However, anger may be harmful and destructive if you cannot control it. Controlling your emotions, particularly your anger, becomes more challenging when you drink. That's because it impairs one's capacity for self-control and internal discipline. Anger and alcohol are more closely related than emotion regulation.

For certain people, anger serves as a coping mechanism. They use their anger as a bulwark against other, more challenging emotions and behaviors. Instead of expressing natural emotions, a person with an alcohol use disorder (AUD) would express fury to avoid dealing with uncomfortable or unfavorable circumstances, including the addiction itself.

Research indicates that alcohol consumption increases aggressiveness. Alcohol plays a major role in around half of all violent crimes that occur in the US. The regular or excessive use of alcohol is referred to as alcohol abuse or alcoholism. Drinking impairs your ability to reason logically and with clarity. It might be harder to control your feelings, affecting your capacity to resist urges.

ADHD stands for attention deficit hyperactivity disorder.

Deficit in Focus Being a neurodevelopmental condition, ADHD is caused by differences in the way the nervous system forms and functions. ADHD is the most common neurodevelopmental disorder in children, affecting an estimated 5 to 7 percent of all school-age children. ADHD frequently manifests before the age of 7, yet symptoms cannot show up until a child is a bit older and encounters more challenging social and academic situations. Children diagnosed with ADHD are more likely to experience learning disabilities, depression, anxiety disorders, and other behavioral disorders such as oppositional defiant disorder.

Adults with ADHD who were diagnosed as children are significantly more likely to suffer from a variety of mental health conditions as well as conditions that could affect important aspects of life, such as relationships, employment, and education. For these reasons, early identification and treatment are essential. Adult ADHD is the term for the problem where some people may not receive a diagnosis of ADHD until they reach adulthood. All ages of people with ADHD may also be irritable and angry.

ODD, or oppositional defiant disorder

Oppositional defiant disorder (ODD) in children is a behavioral condition marked by aggressive and persistent defiance. One in ten children under the age of twelve are predicted to have ODD, with boys outnumbering girls two to one. Typical signs of ODD include impatience, anger, and short fuse. Children with ODD frequently get easily agitated by other people. They might be obstinate and belligerent. Early intervention and therapy are essential since children with untreated ODD may remain challenging and antisocial into adulthood. Their relationships, career opportunities, and overall quality of life may all be impacted by this. Some ODD patients may progress to a more severe conduct disorder (CD), which is marked by violent and aggressive activities that break the law.

Manic episodes

Periods (or episodes) of severe mood disorders that affect behavior, thoughts, and emotions are the hallmarks of bipolar disorder, a mental health condition. Bipolar disorders are primarily classified into two types. Severe mania and depression are common signs of bipolar disorder. Less severe mania linked to bipolar II disorder is called hypomania. These sudden mood changes can range from manic to sad, even though not everyone with bipolar illness experiences depression. Episodes of rage, frustration, and anger are typical in bipolar people.

Periodic explosive illness

Intermittent explosive disorder (IED) is a disorder of impulse control marked by violent outbursts of rage, physical aggression, and verbal abuse. Individuals with IEDs struggle to control their emotional responses to distressing events. During an episode, they could swear at people or animals, damage property, or act impulsively hostile.

Strong outbursts of rage that can last anywhere from a few minutes to half an hour are the main characteristic of IEDs. After that, the person frequently calms down, apologizes, or expresses sorrow for what they did. There may be intervals between episodes of greater intensity and less severe ones. Usually, in late childhood or early adolescence, the sickness first appears. Some common behaviors include fighting, yelling, temper tantrums, physical violence, and throwing objects.

Sadness

Anger is one of the stages of sorrow. Losing your job, going through a divorce or breakup, or the death of a loved one can all cause grief. The targets of the rage could be the deceased person, any other parties involved in the act, or inanimate objects. The agony of losing a loved one may cause you to experience uncontrollable wrath and other anger-related sensations during the rage stage of mourning. One moment, you might be emotionally stable and normal; the next, you might snap at anything or everybody in your way. Other symptoms of mourning include shock, numbness, regret, sadness, loneliness, and dread.

The filth of unfairness

Persecutors can drive anyone insane, as one ancient Israeli King stated in an equally old book of wisdom. The social structure is rife with injustice. Due to widespread racial prejudice, some people experience unfair treatment, such as having less access to jobs and education. Some people are slain or placed under custody for crimes they did not commit.

In many locations, politicians use deceit and lying to get to the top. After that, they use their power to siphon off money from the public coffers for their pals and themselves. The oppressed populations are abandoned to their agony. When faced with pervasive injustice and no consolation, many people become enraged.

Just keep in mind that you're just making things worse for yourself if the injustice, tyranny, and inequity you witness all around you are the source of your rage. Your fury won't make the world right again or bring justice upon those who do injustices.

Accepting things as they are and putting your calm head and energy into trying your best to live in this hostile world is the wisest course of action. The religious mindset, which holds that an all-powerful living force will eventually interfere in human events to end injustice, is highly beneficial. A ship's anchor can be found in faith.

Financial desperation

It's simple to understand how financial difficulties may rob people of a happy existence and force them to live in a constant state of annoyance and rage.

Unceremoniously, some people lost their jobs, and most had no safety nets to help them through life. So, you have the ideal conditions for tense emotion that gives rise to rage and irritable conduct when unemployed people and those without employment fear losing them.

You would assume wealthy people would be immune to anxieties stoked by the economy. They're not. They closely observe the ups and downs of the bulls and bears on the stock market charts with their eyes and ears glued to them. After their big equities market loss, pray that you have nothing to do with them in the morning.

You would agree that people of all social classes can get depressed due to economic concerns. Poverty leads to annoyance and rage.

The amusement sector

They frequently provide audiences with intense amounts of violence in their film narratives. Furthermore, several studies have demonstrated that people, particularly kids, become accustomed to hostility when they are exposed to realistic violence regularly.

In addition to desensitization, people who are often exposed to violent media frequently start to view rage and aggression as legitimate, even honorable, ways to deal with hardship. This is precisely what you see happening in many places of the world right now: a decline in compassion and an increase in fury.

There are a ton of additional elements that support the development of hate and rage in society. Some of them you might recognize. However, what matters most is that you must decide in your heart that harboring anger is too dangerous a habit to pursue. We'll examine the grave consequences of fury in the upcoming chapter of this manual to assist readers in deciding to abstain from it.

THE NEED TO ACKNOWLEDGE ANGER AS NATURAL

An emotional state of frustration, dread, wrath, and self-doubt can precipitate a personal crisis. Given that they are the closest, they might be hostile. Or they might get grumpy and exhausted. An agitation can typically manifest as lethargy, apathy, sadness, slowed sex desire, loss of appetite, and weariness. Even though some of these symptoms may be unsettling, they are typical, expected reactions in persons who have experienced significant life upheavals. Determining and comprehending one's sensations is the first step toward identifying them. Any emotions—usually unpleasant—may be repressed, making them invisible. It's critical to acknowledge these intense emotions, consider their reasons, and find healthy coping mechanisms. Your body and your emotions will be destroyed if you refuse to acknowledge your feelings.

A vital human emotion is rage. Although everyone experiences anger occasionally, how we respond to and manage this emotion is important to us. You may behave differently at work and home and alter how you connect with people if you are frustrated by conflict or challenging circumstances. You ought to be aware of how you handle frustration.

Anger is a powerful emotion; many people associate anger with negative things. We would rather be angry when we experience rejection, disqualification, frustration, or injury in challenging circumstances. We must experience irritation in these situations because it helps us to care for ourselves and recognize our identity. When we channel our anger constructively, it may provide us with drive and vigor. But we must also learn to restrain our anger and discourage harmful behavior. Not other people or situations, but rather how we react to what is happening is what irritates us. Because each person is unique, they all react to stressful situations differently. While some people may look distant and hostile, others may stay composed. We must be aware of our anger. Ignoring it also makes us prone to exploding at the first sign of excessive thinking. Repressed fury can be just as problematic as being "out of control." Both may have an impact on one's health and well-beingwellbeing.

Wrath is associated with negativity when compared to positive feelings like joy, excitement, and hope. Disdain for outrage may stem from national, cultural, and religious sources and an obvious illustration of their occasionally negative effects, such as hostility and violence. I think we will have a better feeling without indignation. However, anger is becoming more and more beneficial to humankind and has been shown to improve mental health, cognitive scientists, evolutionary psychologists, and psychologists. When considered optimally, all sentiments are sufficient under specific circumstances to offer the resources to work effectively toward the intended objective. For example, tension and anxiety motivate us to work hard. We can express our gratitude for what we've missed by letting others know that we require help to survive and recover from sadness, which can be cathartic. Like mild to moderate anger fosters beneficial growth, strong or persistent anger may harm our wellbeing. Anger is not only physical. It frequently provides knowledge that helps us better relate to the world around us and ourselves. If we interpret irritation as a signal, we can adjust our response to our circumstances.

Here is a list of advantages that indignation can offer when the intensity of the emotion is high enough.

Anger Is Meant To Encourage Survival

Emotions evolved to protect us. Frustration is the root of our response to combat, which originated as a means of defending oneself against an adversary or threat. Our natural need to survive and protect ourselves from harm includes the capacity for wrath. Anger sharpens our focus and increases our awareness of dangers. Our instinct is to defend ourselves and strike back easily and ferocity when someone confronts or harms us.

The Release of Anger Is Calm

When you are upset, you experience both emotional and physical discomfort. Anger spurs you to action when you are in pain, both physically and emotionally. Hence, frustration enables you to ease discomfort by releasing physical tension and relaxing your "nerves." For this reason, you can respond angrily at first and then feel at ease again.

Anger Gives You a Feeling of Control

An intense need for power is linked to wrath. Anger protects our own, making us feel wonderful rather than helpless. To increase expenses or withhold incentives from others to improve our welfare is the object of outrage. To fulfill their desires and control their destiny, those who appropriately feel and express their rage are in a better position than those who hide their rage. It's crucial to use caution to avoid letting your feelings of control or rage divert you.

Anger Gives Us Energy

Life's perspective is that we both intimidate and assault people to defend ourselves. Outrage defends us when someone tries to harm us. This gives us the will and willpower to defeat a more formidable foe. As Richard Davidson states, anger may mobilize resources, improve alertness, and push for the removal of obstacles in our path to success—especially when the anger is isolated from the possibility of harm or destruction.

Anger Drives Us to Find Solutions to Issues

We may become agitated when we feel that situations are beyond our control. Frustration pushes us to take action and solve problems when things aren't going as they should and need to. We become angry when a human (or anything else) or a barrier obstructs our needs. It teaches us how to handle obstacles and problems while pursuing our goals.

Anger Draws Our Attention to Injustice

We frequently become agitated when our liberties are violated, threatened, mistreated, or oppressed. An internal control mechanism known as rage alerts us when someone has treated us unfairly or incorrectly. Anger fosters interpersonal relationships: "You should treat me fairly." If not, it would come at a heavy price." Taking global justice issues head-on can deter people from taking advantage of others. Such outrage will increase the societal cost of misconduct and bring beneficial social change.

Anger Pushes Us Toward Our Objectives

Anger drives us to pursue our ultimate objectives and rewards. Anger appears when we don't receive what we want and shows that we are straying from our intended course. Anger tries to destroy everything in the way of achieving our goals. It gives us motivation and inspiration to pursue our objectives and ideals.

Angry People Are Optimistic

Unexpectedly, elation can give rise to rage. This will assist in reflecting on our goals rather than only focusing on suffering, provocation, and victimization. The revenge plan is based on what is realistic, not improbable. Even in moments of frustration, we remain optimistic about our capacity to respond, alter the course of events, and shift from undesirable to desirable situations.

Controlling Your Anger

rage management is a crucial skill everyone who experiences rage must acquire. As implied by the term, anger management is learning to manage and control your anger in a way that doesn't negatively impact you or those around you. It involves discovering healthy ways to control your emotions so that neither you nor those around you suffer. Although it may appear difficult, anger management is fairly easy; all you need is commitment and perseverance. If you want to learn how to control your anger, you have to be committed and adamant about wanting to control it.

You must acknowledge that anger is an issue before learning how to manage it. Some people don't bother trying to learn how to control their anger because they don't understand that it's a problem that needs to be addressed. Furthermore, they don't think that they are the ones who are having problems. Rather, they try to place the blame for their problems elsewhere. Therefore, you must acknowledge it as an issue that must be solved immediately. The first step in learning to regulate and control our emotions is to become self-aware.

Determining the cause of the issue comes next after realizing it is a problem. Thus, look within and pose the following queries to yourself:

"What makes me angry?"

"What is the reason for my rage?"

"What can I do better when I'm upset?"

"What impact has it had on my interpersonal relationships?"

"Am I pleased with this response?"

"Why can't I be logical instead of emotional? Why is this strong emotion controlling me?"

When done sitting down, this kind of questioning is a crucial stage since it may help you pinpoint the source of your anger.

The next step is understanding how to overcome the sensation or reason causing you to project anger after identifying it. You must be resilient and set your mind to doing this. You have mastered the art of managing and controlling your anger when you can face the underlying emotion that causes it and grasp its reins. To be resilient, you have to be able to take charge of a circumstance that could easily make you angry and stop it from doing so. You have to become adept at handling your anxieties and uncertainties. You must learn to let go of every unpleasant feeling you think makes you angry. You must understand that it's better to learn how to move on from upsetting circumstances than to get enraged and resentful about them. Here are a few doable strategies for learning how to control your rage.

Acclimate yourself to your anger signals: It gets easier to recognize when you will have an angry fit or outburst once you are aware of your anger signals. The fundamental indicators include an increase in heart rate and pulse and tingling in some people's palms. Seeing any of these signs indicates that you are becoming more irate and may soon lose it. You can prepare for it and avoid being surprised if you know it is approaching.

2. WAIT A WHILE before REACTING: This is like putting yourself through a time-out; it means you must learn to control yourself before exploding in a rage. Try to stop yourself when you feel

your wrath rising, and count to ten before you respond. Counting from 1 to 10 will assist your growing rage to subside as quickly as it appeared.

3. TAKE DEEP AND SLOW BREATHES: Your breathing gets erratic and irregular when you are about to have an angry outburst. So, before you do anything, you must learn to control your breathing. Controlling your breathing not only calms you down and helps you combat angry emotions but also preserves your rationality, allowing you to reason sensibly and coherently.

4. RELAXATION OF MUSCLE. Try your hardest to let your muscles relax when you're upset. Opening your fist is the

first step in accomplishing this. When you're upset, clenching your hand seems to be a reflex motion that mentally prepares you for a fight. Your brain receives messages from relaxed muscles that indicate you are in control of the situation and at ease. You're more likely to behave logically than emotionally if you perform this small action. You would have subdued a fierce and strong emotion in the easiest method possible.

These actions aid in the management and containment of sudden, intense outbursts of anger; however, if you are the kind that has frequent episodes of anger, more actions are required. Here are some more clever techniques for developing self-control and managing your anger:

Casual activities: Regular exercise releases feel-good chemicals like dopamine and serotonin into your body, which improves your mood and reduces your impulsivity. This is why exercising is a wonderful approach to learning anger management. Exercise is also a fantastic way to reduce stress, so it will be a great approach to control your anger if it is brought on by stress.

RELAXATION methods: Using relaxation methods is another method for teaching anger management. To de-stress and meditate, set aside some quiet time for yourself. By doing these, you become more adept at managing stress and frustration, which reduces your likelihood of becoming irate.

Talk about your emotions: Confer your feelings with a close friend or family member. It could be preferable for you to start an anger notebook if you are shy or private and don't want to talk to someone about your feelings. You can freely express yourself and write down your feelings by keeping an anger journal. Doing this may ensure that you don't repress your emotions or express them harmfully.

Don't hold grudges: This calls for you to develop the ability to let go of your resentment. Never let thoughts that the world is unfair or that people are against you to dominate your thinking. Get rid of ideas that make you angry and open your mind to clarity and purity.

Act assertively: Being assertive entails learning to achieve your goals while considering other people's sentiments.

It may be time to get professional assistance if you find it difficult to control your anger using these methods.

Be Aware Of Your Triggers

Knowing what makes you angry and how to control it is important. Although being mindful helps you learn to regulate your anger even in the face of numerous situations, people, and things that can make you angry, achieving this elevated level of awareness and self-control takes time.

You are now a novice in mindfulness and have only recently become aware of your condition. It will take a while to reach the point when you fully know your emotions and self. You must avoid things that make you feel anxious, frustrated, or angry until then. You must learn to recognize your triggers if you want to do it.

Here's how to go about doing that.

1: Determine What Makes You Mad

Try the following to figure out what makes you angry:

1. Take a close look at yourself and stay current. If you catch yourself displaying one of the earlier-identified signs or symptoms of rage, find out exactly what went wrong before it. Have you met someone who has offended you? Have you seen anything that made you angry? Were you engaged in any activities that made you angry?

2. Consider the following elements to determine what makes you angry:

Action: Reflect on your behavior when you felt angry and irritated. Before your episodes of agitation, what were you doing, or are you doing? For example, when I became aware that I was an angry person, I discovered that the majority of the time, my agitation stemmed from thinking about bad experiences from my past.

PERSONS: When you're angry, who are you connecting with, talking to, or surrounding yourself with? Some individuals bring out your greatest qualities, while others bring out your worst. See if you are being subjected to the latter by someone.

Place: When you become aware of your anger, where are you sitting or standing? Some locations also make you angry. Amy, 38, struggled with her anger a year ago. Her boyfriend's breakup with her at a coffee shop was the catalyst for her issue ever since she intensely disliked coffee shops and became irrationally angry if she spotted a pair there.

Emotion status: When you get angry, pay attention to your feelings. Anger frequently stems from another emotion you are experiencing. There are times when stress, hurt feelings, or frustration when things do not go your way cause you to become furious. You can control your anger if you know the emotional condition that leads to it.

Keep a two- to the three-week diary of these triggers to better understand them. When you feel angry, write it down in your journal and investigate the issue to determine what exactly set you off. You'll better understand your anger triggers by the end of two or three weeks. Once you are aware of it, do these actions:

2: Set Your Triggers Aside for a While

Use your judgment to temporarily avoid all of your anger triggers to make sure your anger doesn't get worse. Doing this lets you become more attentive to the problem without worsening it. Ignore everyone, everything, and everything that makes you feel angry or anxious for a few weeks.

If a coworker irritates you, avoid interacting with him and work from the comfort of your cubicle instead. Avoid watching TV for a few days if you find reading news about your nation's awful political situation upsetting. This aids in preventing furious situations, which in turn aids in your ability to de-stress.

In the interim, pay attention to the many thought patterns that elicit rage. Using this technique, you can control the various emotional states that lead to rage.

3: Recognize the Thoughts That Fuel Your Rage

Some mental processes exacerbate and fuel your rage.

To permanently overcome chronic anger, you need to become aware of mental patterns like these:

Mental reading: You can read minds. Thus, you draw inferences and make assumptions using this ability. Take phrases like "I think you don't like me" or "I know you feel I annoy you too much," for example.

Saying such things to someone just makes you angry and irritates them (nobody likes mind readers). As you may know, it can enrage you when someone takes offense at your assumptions or inferences about them.

As my previous story demonstrates, when I struggled with anger management, I used to assume my partner's opinions about me, which frequently resulted in heated disputes.

Overgeneralizing: Making blanket claims like "You always disrespect me" or "You never pay attention to me" hurts and depresses you. This is another negative thought habit that fuels your rage.

Partying in the blame game: Assigning blame to others is an unwholesome behavior that intensifying your fury. One of your numerous anger triggers is probably the habit of blaming others for your aggravation and wrath.

You are a habitual blame game player if you frequently say statements like "You trigger my anger," "You did this/that wrong just to upset me," or "It is your fault that I became angry." By assigning blame, you absolve yourself of accountability for your rage. You never take your toxic feelings seriously when you don't own up to them.

Become aware of these mental patterns and investigate their sources to prevent yourself from becoming a victim of chronic rage. This aids in the management of the various negative feelings that lead to rage.

Every time someone abuses you, you might find you can "read minds." This insight enables you to recognize how melancholy feeds rage. You must control your sadness before you can tackle your rage issue.

Go on to the next tactic after you have a greater knowledge and awareness of your triggers.

The Various Kinds of Anger

Although it may be simple to ignore or lump all forms of rage together, there are a variety of forms and profiles of anger that people might experience. Many of these anger profile kinds are related to one another, and depending on what's going on in your environment or what set off your emotional outburst, you may transition from one form of anger to another in a short amount of time or longer. Let's examine common sorts of anger and how to recognize them.

ANGER IN PAUSE. Silence or repression are the hallmarks of resistant rage, another name for passive fury. This kind of rage is either ignored or tried to be contained within, yet it might show itself as rude remarks or passive-aggressive words directed at the individual in question or at others in the vicinity. Passive anger may be displayed if you have been displeased or agitated with someone or something but choose to ignore it or simply voice your opinion to someone else.

It can be difficult to control passive or resistant anger, and research has shown that it can be harmful to one's health, particularly if untreated for an extended length of time. Psychotherapist Peter Sacco, Ph.D., of New York, said in an interview with EverydayHealth.com, "Your body is tense all the time when you keep the feelings all bottled up." Your immune system deteriorates, and you become more susceptible to skin disorders, temporomandibular joint dysfunction, cancer, heart disease, and osteoarthritis. This kind of person frequently snaps at some point."

Many people could employ passive anger, also known as passive-aggressive behavior, since society often disapproves of overt displays of rage or confrontation. Signe Whitson L.S.W. writes in a piece for Psychology Today that "Anger is a normal, natural human emotion." In actuality, it's among the most fundamental human experiences. However, many of us are indoctrinated at a young age that rage is bad. We discover that to be considered "good," we must suppress our honest self-expression and bury our anger during a stage of emotional development when we are most vulnerable to social pressure from parents, guardians, and teachers. People don't simply lose their anger when they discover they can't communicate openly, honestly, and directly with others. Instead, many of us pick up other, discreet, and socially acceptable methods to communicate it, frequently through passive-aggressive actions."

Whitson further points out that passive-aggressive behavior may be the simpler solution in many circumstances. In the current era of Race to the Top, Common

Core, and standardized testing, social skills education is frequently cut from a young person's official education. Nonetheless, research after research demonstrates that specialized teaching in "soft" skills like relationship building, assertiveness, and emotion control is just as important to a child's growth as any "hardcore" math and reading knowledge. Not every individual who exhibits passive-aggressive behavior is considered to be passive-aggressive. For instance, a husband who usually has open and honest communication with his spouse might not have the resources one weekend to turn down her request to have a leaky faucet fixed, so he makes a lot of excuses to put it off. The man is not always passive aggressive, but when unwinding and avoiding conflict with his spouse are his main concerns on this particular day, he selects passive aggression as the easy way to act."

Variable fury. Intermittent explosive disorder is intimately linked to this kind of anger as well. The hallmark of volatile anger is erratic outbursts of rage that are disproportionately enormous or exaggerated in relation to the situation or trigger that sparked them.

According to EverydayHealth.com, people with specific illnesses related to substance misuse or men are more likely to exhibit this anger profile. Those who struggle with substance misuse and men are slightly more likely to experience volatile anger. Anger of this kind puts a person at risk for property damage, violence against others, self-harm, and interpersonal interaction problems. If someone close to you exhibits this kind of rage, it's crucial to get expert assistance and exercise caution."

Professional treatment is frequently necessary for volatile rage, particularly in cases where intermittent explosive disorder is identified. They usually strike unexpectedly, with little to no notice, and last less than thirty minutes. In between violent outbursts, there may be less severe verbal outbursts. You might be impulsive, violent, irritated, or persistently furious most of the time. Anger, impatience, heightened energy, racing thoughts, tingling, tremors, palpitations, and tightness in the chest can all precede or follow an aggressive episode."

PERMANENT ANGER. Chronic rage is anger that persists for an extended time without being controlled or addressed. Anger can result in various health issues, most notably a weakened immune system, when it becomes a habit for the individual. An individual who experiences chronic anger is described by Peter Sacco, Ph., as "someone who develops anger as a habit." When he or she wakes up, he or she is furious and angrily proceeds from one item to the next, mentally preparing themselves for another challenging day. He or she is constantly searching for a cause for ire. If left untreated, this is the kind of person who gets into legal problems or isolates themselves from friends and family."

According to Mike Brundant, author of "NLP Discoveries" on PsychCentral.com, "A high-fat diet, obesity, and smoking are not the only risk factors for early death and chronic disease—chronic anger is so harmful to your body that it may even surpass these factors." Even worse, nobody seemed to know how to handle it. Some advise you shouldn't repress your anger because doing so would simply exacerbate the physical harm. Others argue that you shouldn't vent it either because doing so will worsen bodily harm! Anger is frustrating.

Heart conditions, high blood pressure, migraines and persistent headaches, skin conditions, digestive issues, exhaustion, chronic pain, and alcohol or drug addiction are just a few of the consequences associated with chronic rage.

Furious Anger

You are about to lose control and go into full-blown fury. You just can't stand it any longer. You no longer care about other people's sentiments or your environment.

You feel this rage as it arises and as it continuously intensifies. Your brain enters fight-or-flight mode when perceiving threat, injustice, or attack. If you enter fight mode, you can find yourself in a full-blown rage, screaming, cursing, and prepared for a physical altercation.

This is transient craziness, this exploding wrath. It frequently leads to you saying the wrong thing to the wrong person and acting incorrectly. Once things calm down, it leaves you in a mess. You can discover that relationships are irreparable and that people won't accept your apology later. In this instance, any potential future relationship with this person was shattered by the fury you allowed to take over you.

Waiting it out is the greatest way to deal with intense anger. That's the opposite of avoidance fury, which calls for immediate attention. Anger reactions, according to experts, occur within two seconds after the incident. Count to ten whenever you sense your wrath building and tell yourself again, "I am in control of my anger." It makes sense that reciting this phrase aloud will remove a significant amount of the tension that is building inside of you. Tell the other person they are making you furious and that your anger grows after being calm for at least 30 seconds. The important thing is to address them with objectivity rather than personality. After doing this, you'll see how simple it is to defuse a situation.

Persistent Anger

This is when you are irritated and pulled along by the same thing every day of the week, but you choose to ignore or deflect it. This is more inconvenient because it typically occurs when it is inappropriate to express rage. It might be that your colleague frequently types loudly on his keyboard. For that reason, there's no cause to be angry with someone, but over time, it could irritate you to the point where you get enraged.

It agitates, snaps, and makes you grumpy but keeps you from losing it and blowing up. This can make you constantly unhappy, and if left untreated, it can also hurt your relationships and general health.

Discover what is upsetting you and why it makes you feel that way. Occasionally, we become enraged due to a background issue that goes unnoticed. Recognize what triggers your swearing or curing, even if it's just minor irritations. These minor irritations have the potential to accumulate over months or even years to cause enduring rage. Inform your colleague that you're losing your mind over his typing. Admit to your partner that you get angry when they leave their clothes in the open. Anger can be readily avoided in these instances with appropriate communication and investigation.

Aggressive Passive Anger

Though you prefer to avoid conflict, you want to express your feelings. Although you don't want to enter a confrontation, you also don't deserve to be treated lightly. Usually, it begins when you're irritated but don't want to act dramatic. But this is just your underlying hostility radiating outward in waves.

You begin to feel angry but ignore it and find other outlets for your feelings. Usually, in a more subdued manner, making others uncomfortable in your presence. They wonder why you are always so resentful and sad, yet they can understand why you are acting a little strange or off.

In actuality, you aren't voicing your rage in this situation sufficiently. This is too indirect, just as the exploding anger is too direct. You must learn to voice your concerns when they arise and quit being silent. The first step is to realize that a confrontation won't always result in a fight or quarrel. Most people use logic to address their problems. Tell the other person, "It bothers me; stop doing this." Would you please stop?

By doing this, you can ensure no conflict while addressing your need to express your disapproval of the situation. Don't sugarcoat the truth. Don't be gloomy and assume that people will just get why you're angry. Others may not understand why you are upset since you are sensitive and easily offended. Speaking about and addressing the issues will immediately improve your emotional condition.

Irony

Often, your best defense is sarcasm. In essence, what is coming out of your mouth is acid. Because you were raised to believe that showing anger in public is bad, you are accustomed to and at ease with using sarcasm. It is much better to inject a dash of humor in there than to be confrontational. Comedy usually targets someone else, and as long as it's not you, it's okay.

The issue is that it occasionally has the potential to injure and offend other individuals. Although it might not offend you, it might, and this could damage your relationships.

It's okay to occasionally make snap judgments, but you should strive to communicate your emotions more honestly. Tell the person who is late that you find it extremely annoying and ask them to understand. Please arrive on time the next time.

Not only will you resolve problems far more quickly by speaking and addressing the matter directly, but you'll also build stronger relationships with people overall. Not everybody is accustomed to irony.

Self-Mutilation

In this case, the person turns their rage inward. You are the reason why things go wrong every time. You blame yourself for everything that goes wrong, and you are especially harsh on yourself when others close to you disappoint you.

When your partner ignores you, you can think, "I am worthless," rather than telling them how uncomfortable it is for you, I can see why my partner accuses me.

Your low self-esteem causes you to focus your rage inward. You find it simpler to acknowledge that you are to blame than someone else. When things go terrible, you eventually start to believe that you are the one with bad luck and that everything awful that happens to you is meant to happen.

An unhealthy self-destruction may result from this. You naturally start to see yourself as less complete when you place the responsibility on yourself. You'll feel depressed, unmotivated, exhausted, and without anything to look forward to. Not to mention the connections you break off, the respect you lose, or the job promotion you don't get.

The first step in healing this illness is to quit blaming yourself. You have to learn to stand up for your team, even if you are the one who is really at fault. In actuality, you should target the people who initially incited your rage. Recognize that the individual who first brought about the catastrophe should bear the guilt, not you. Begin mentally repeating affirmations daily. Have faith in your significance, uniqueness, and deservingness of love and respect. Find a reputable shrink if you require medical assistance. This kind of self-deprecating and self-blame behavior will only work to undermine your current circumstances.

A FEW COMMON M A"PƎNPE TƎN MĐNAGEMENT REGíRDÁNG ANGER

• Although anger should not be repressed, expressing it aggressively is not a healthy alternative, particularly if it is aimed at real people.

• A few individuals utilize anger as a tool for gaining respect. That doesn't hold up since anger is more likely to incite fear and mistrust than it is to win respect.

• In terms of management, some individuals believe that anger cannot be controlled. Anger may indeed be controlled; we always have a choice in expressing our anger.

Ultimately, anger is something that some of us believe ought to be suppressed. That's not realistic. Anger is irrational; it will surface when we are pushed too far. The likelihood of experiencing anger frequently results in the necessity of expressing it appropriately.

Equation that is not properly controlled or managed

- We damage our relationships with our significant others, who we may be harming emotionally or physically as a result of improperly controlled anger.

- We damage our friendships and connections with friends and colleagues because we become frightening and intimidating; we don't come off as someone easy to deal with.

- Anger that isn't properly addressed destroys you mentally and physically. We experience stress more frequently, which raises our risk of heart disease, diabetes, stroke, and a host of other illnesses. We also lose our ability to reason, demonstrate appropriately, and solve problems.

www.ingramcontent.com/pod-product-compliance
Lightning Source LLC
Chambersburg PA
CBHW052133110526
44591CB00012B/1698